Veterans Day

by Meredith Dash

ABDO
NATIONAL HOLIDAYS
Kids

www.abdopublishing.com

Published by Abdo Kids, a division of ABDO, PO Box 398166, Minneapolis, Minnesota 55439.

Copyright © 2015 by Abdo Consulting Group, Inc. International copyrights reserved in all countries. No part of this book may be reproduced in any form without written permission from the publisher.

Printed in the United States of America, North Mankato, Minnesota.

052014

092014

THIS BOOK CONTAINS
RECYCLED MATERIALS

Photo Credits: AP Images, Corbis, Shutterstock, Thinkstock, © Anthony Correia p.cover, © Warren Price Photography p.1, © spirit of america p.17, 21 / Shutterstock.com

Production Contributors: Teddy Borth, Jennie Forsberg, Grace Hansen

Design Contributors: Candice Keimig, Laura Rask, Dorothy Toth

Library of Congress Control Number: 2013952081

Cataloging-in-Publication Data

Dash, Meredith.

 Veterans Day / Meredith Dash.

  p. cm. -- (National holidays)

ISBN 978-1-62970-048-9 (lib. bdg.)

Includes bibliographical references and index.

1. Veterans Day--Juvenile literature.   I. Title.

394.264--dc23

            2013952081

Table of Contents

Veterans Day

November 11, 1918 was

an important day. Fighting

in World War I ended.

It was called **Armistice Day**.

7

It became a holiday

on May 13, 1938.

9

The years went on. More

people fought for America.

There were more veterans.

November 11 became

Veterans Day in 1954.

It honored **veterans**

of all wars.

13

A law was made in 1968.

All **national holidays**

moved to Mondays.

People were unhappy.

They wanted Veterans Day

to be on November 11.

17

When We Celebrate

President Gerald Ford agreed. In 1975 he signed a law. It returned Veterans Day to November 11.

19

Who We Celebrate

Veterans Day is a day

to thank our veterans.

They served to keep us safe.

21

More Facts

- President Wilson proclaimed November 11th **Armistice Day** in 1919.

- President Eisenhower signed the bill changing the holiday's name to Veterans Day.

- America's Parade in New York City is the largest celebration of Veterans Day in the United States.

Glossary

Armistice Day – the armistice signed between the allies and Germany to end World War I.

national holiday – a special event celebrated by a country.

veteran – a person who has served in the armed forces.

World War I – a war fought in Europe from 1914 to 1918.

Index

abdokids.com

Use this code to log on to abdokids.com and access crafts, games, videos and more!

Abdo Kids Code:
NVK0489

24